The
DOG LOVERS'
Guides

Rottweiler

The DOG LOVERS' *Guides*

Beagle
Boxer
Bulldog
Cavalier King Charles Spaniel
Chihuahua
Cocker Spaniel
Dachshund
French Bulldog
German Shepherd
Golden Retriever
Labrador Retriever
Miniature Schnauzer
Poodle
Pug
Rottweiler
Siberian Husky
Shih Tzu
Yorkshire Terrier

Rottweiler

By Julie Johnson

Mason Crest
450 Parkway Drive, Suite D
Broomall, PA 19008
www.masoncrest.com

Printed and bound in the United States of America.

Series ISBN: 978-1-4222-3848-6
Hardback ISBN: 978-1-4222-3860-8
EBook ISBN: 978-1-4222-7939-7

First printing
1 3 5 7 9 8 6 4 2

Cover photograph by Erik Mandre/Dreamstime.com.

Library of Congress Cataloging-in-Publication Data is on file with the publisher.

QR Codes disclaimer

You may gain access to certain third-party content ("Third-Party Sites") by scanning and using the QR Codes that appear in this publication (the "QR Codes"). We do not operate or control in any respect any information, products, or services on such Third-Party Sites linked to by us via the QR Codes included in this publication, and we assume no responsibility for any materials you may access using the QR Codes. Your use of the QR Codes may be subject to terms, limitations, or restrictions set forth in the applicable terms of use or otherwise established by the owners of the Third-Party Sites. Our linking to such Third-Party Sites via the QR Codes does not imply an endorsement or sponsorship of such Third-Party Sites, or the information, products, or services offered on or through the Third-Party Sites, nor does it imply an endorsement or sponsorship of this publication by the owners of such Third-Party Sites.

Contents

Key Icons to Look For

Sidebars: This boxed material within the main text allows readers to build knowledge, gain insights, explore possibilities, and broaden their perspectives by weaving together additional information to provide realistic and holistic perspectives.

Educational Videos: Readers can view videos by scanning our QR codes, providing them with additional educational content to supplement the text. Examples include news coverage, moments in history, speeches, iconic moments, and much more!

Series Glossary of Key Terms: This back-of-the-book glossary contains terminology used throughout this series. Words found here increase the reader's ability to read and comprehend higher-level books and articles in this field.

Chapter 1

Introducing the Rottweiler

Noble, powerful, impressive in appearance, the Rottweiler is a breed like no other. He has strong guarding instincts but is loyal and loving to his family, and is always eager to please. This is a dog who loves to work; he is highly intelligent and that means mental stimulation is essential for him. Among family and friends, he is laidback and likes nothing better than to make everyone laugh by playing the clown.

The Rottweiler's behavior is self-assured, steady, and fearless. This is not a breed for the faint-hearted, but if you have time to spend with your Rottweiler, socializing him and training him, he will be an outstanding family companion.

The feature that attracts me most about this breed is the loyalty Rottweilers show to their family, and the undying love they are capable of giving. I am also drawn to their somewhat clownish nature; not a day goes by when I do not laugh at the antics of at least one of my own four Rottweilers.

Family companion

If you are thinking of getting one of these magnificent creatures, or have already owned one, be prepared to be hooked for life. Many people who start out with one dog will end up being a multi-Rott-weiler household.

This is a relatively easy breed to care for. His handsome short coat needs minimal grooming, and, as long as you are careful during his vulnerable growing stage, he thrives on a routine of regular, varied exercise. With good management—and good luck—most Rottwei-lers will live past the age of ten.

Rottweilers get along well with other dogs, and adapt to living with other, smaller breeds. In most cases, a mixed pair—male and female—will get along best, but for this to work successfully both dogs should be neutered. Same-sex pairs have a tendency to squab-

ble, and this can lead to serious problems if it is not nipped in the bud.

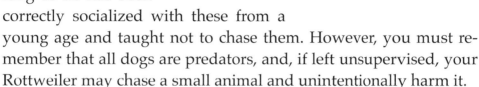

A Rottweiler will live happily alongside cats, rabbits, guinea pigs, horses, and just about any other animal, as long as he has been correctly socialized with these from a young age and taught not to chase them. However, you must remember that all dogs are predators, and, if left unsupervised, your Rottweiler may chase a small animal and unintentionally harm it.

The Rottweiler sees himself as family protector; he will be tolerant of children, and may bond closely with them if mutual respect is established at an early stage. Bear in mind that a cuddly Rottweiler puppy will grow into a large, powerful adult, so it is essential to supervise interactions with small children—no matter how trustworthy your Rottweiler appears to be.

At the other end of the age spectrum, the Rottweiler may not be the best choice for those getting on in years, or people with physical disabilities. Obviously, good training is the key to having a well-behaved dog no matter his size—but the sheer power of the Rottweiler may be too much of a challenge.

The versatile Rottweiler

This is a highly intelligent breed who needs to use his brain. During World Wars I and II, Rottweilers were put into service in various roles, working as messenger, draft, and guard dogs. Today, they are often used as search and rescue dogs, assistance dogs, guide dogs for the blind, therapy dogs, and guard and police dogs.

However, the vast majority of Rottweilers are companion dogs, and although they fit this role admirably, most pet dogs require extra mental stimulation.

You can provide this in many different ways, from teaching basic obedience and inventing new tricks and exercises for your Rottweiler, to getting involved in more advanced training. If you are interested in competing in one of the canine sports, such as obedience, agility, working trials, schutzhund, or tracking, look no further! The Rottweiler excels in all these disciplines, and working closely with your Rottweiler will enrich your relationship and build a closer bond.

Rottweiler history

The origin of Rottweilers is not well documented, but it is believed that they are descended from Roman cattle dogs or drovers, making them one of the oldest herding breeds in history.

The Roman legions would have traveled with their meat "on the hoof," and therefore needed dogs to herd the cattle, as well as guard the livestock at night against dangers such as wolves or cattle rus-

tlers. One route the army traveled was through Württemberg and on to the small market town of Rottweil. This town was populated by the Romans between the years 81 and 96, during which time they rebuilt it—erecting stone buildings with red tile roofs on the most important ones. The town got the name Rote Wil (meaning Red Villa), which eventually became Rottweil.

Over time, this region became an important area for raising and selling cattle, and the descendants of the Roman cattle dogs mixed with local dogs, and other large breeds the Romans met on their travels. These included Molosser dogs from Britain and the Netherlands, which proved their worth in both driving and protecting the cattle from robbers and wild animals. The butchers and cattle dealers found this big herding dog ideal, and from this grew a trade, based in Rottweil, in purposely bred working dogs. The dogs who came from Rottweil were, of course, called Rottweilers.

The Swiss connection

Roman droving dogs also settled in Switzerland, and their characteristics were altered to suit the particular area they populated. These dogs are known as Sennenhunds, four of which include the Appenzeller, the Entlebucher, the Bernese Mountain Dog (pictured here), and the Greater Swiss Mountain Dog. It is believed that the Rottweiler is distantly related to the Sennenhunds and, indeed, when you study the breed standards for these dogs, you can see similarities to the Rottweiler of today.

The all-around working dog

The Rottweiler was first and foremost used for herding cattle and pigs, although dogs of this type were also used for herding sheep. It was a hard task to move the animals and to keep them together at the same time. The work required a strong dog with plenty of stamina, both mentally and physically, but who also had the energy and courage to impose his will on obstinate animals.

Rottweiler history

Reliable, calm, full of confidence and physical strength, the Rottweiler knew how to get his job done. He would move the cattle by using his physical strength and weight to lean against them—a trait that can often be seen in their descendants as they lean into you for petting. The more rebellious animals would be nipped at the heels until they moved.

The many qualities of these dogs quickly made them sought after for a wide variety of jobs. Known as the Rottweiler Metzgerhunds (Rottweil's butchers' dogs), they were employed not only to drive cattle, but also for pulling the carts of farmers, butchers, bakers, and peddlers.

In addition, the Rottweiler was an incredible guard dog. Cattle dealers may have tucked the payment for their herds into the collars of their dogs for the journey home, because there would have been few people brave enough to challenge these tough, courageous dogs.

However, by the end of the 19th century, the railroad became the main way stock was moved to market, and a new law in Germany banned driving cattle using dogs. Donkeys were now being used to pull carts as well. As a result, the Rottweiler was largely neglected by the people of Rottweil. The numbers dwindled until, by 1900, there was only one bitch to be found in Rottweil itself.

Rediscovering the breed

At the beginning of the 20th century, the Rottweiler was close to extinction. But the drive and character of the breed came to its rescue.

In 1910, the Rottweiler was officially recognized as the fourth dog breed of the German Police Dog Association. The first two Rottweiler recruits were Max von der Strahlenberg and Flock von Hamburg. This new role enabled the breed to flourish once again.

The first Rottweiler club in Germany, the Deutscher Rottweiler-Klub (DRK, German Rottweiler Club), was formed in January 1907, followed by the creation of the Süddeutscher Rottweiler-Klub (SDRK, South German Rottweiler Club) in April of the same year. The DRK registered around 500 Rottweilers, the SDRK some 3,000 Rottweilers. The goals of the two clubs were different. The DRK wanted to produce working dogs and the SDRK tried to produce a

uniform look, according to the breed standard.

The various German Rottweiler clubs amalgamated in 1921 to form the Allgemeiner Deutscher Rottweiler-Klub (ADRK), which is recognized world-wide as the home club of the Rottweiler.

The Rottweiler goes global

The outstanding qualities of the Rottweiler have been universally recognized, and throughout the world the breed is valued as a show dog, a working dog, and a companion.

The first Rottweiler in the United States was probably brought in by German immigrant Otto Denny in 1929. Denny recorded the first litter born in the United States in the German Stud Book in September of 1930.

The American Kennel Club first registered a Rottweiler in 1931 when a bitch was imported from Germany by August Knecht, followed by a dog named Arras von Gerbermuhle.

The outbreak of World War II put a stop to further development, and progress was slow for many years, with only a few imports from their native Germany. However, that changed dramatically from the 1960s onwards, when the breed quite literally soared in popularity. This is seen most dramatically in U.S. statistics: Only 58 Rottweilers were registered with the AKC in 1958, but that figure had grown to over 100,000 by the 1990s. The Rottweiler became the most popular dog in America. Some fine show dogs and working dogs were produced, along with companion dogs of good character.

However, too many Rottweilers were bred to meet the growing demand, with no regard for their suitability as companion dogs.

Temperament began to suffer. This powerful, fearless dog began to attract bad publicity, as more and more people acquired dogs without understanding how much training and socialization is essential for this breed.

The work of dedicated breeders and Rottweiler enthusiasts helped spread a better understanding of the breed, and address any concerns about temperament. Today, Rottweilers are known for having a very calm disposition, which make them excellent companion animals and family protectors.

Rottweilers are also once again recognized as ideal working dogs. They are used in the United States as guard and police dogs; in Germany by the police, customs, and army; in Denmark mainly by the police; in Switzerland by the customs authority; and in Norway for mountain rescue work. They are also used as border guards in many countries, because they tend to work silently.

In 2016, Rottweilers ranked ninth in popularity among the breeds and varieties registered by the AKC, and it has consistently been in the top ten.

Chapter 2

What Should a Rottweiler Look Like?

For each recognized breed of dog, there is a breed standard, which is drawn up by breed specialists to create a picture in words of the "perfect" dog. It describes the mental and physical characteristics that a breed needs to perform the function for which it was developed, and it describes the breed's looks, movement, and temperament.

Breeders strive to produce a dog who most closely conforms to the breed standard, and at dog shows, judges examine the dogs and place them according to how closely each dog compares with their own interpretation of the standard.

Dogs shows are not just beauty contests; judges are looking for soundness of mind and body. The dogs who win in the show ring

are highly sought after for breeding, and they will be responsible for producing future generations of Rottweilers.

General appearance

A medium to large breed, the Rottweiler is a powerful dog. His size and build demonstrates great strength, agility, and endurance. These traits would have been required to work cattle, which would probably have been wilder than modern-day livestock.

Characteristics and temperament

The Rottweiler is a calm and self-confident dog. He will have an inherent desire to guard both his home and family. He is good-natured and should not be nervous, shy, or too excitable. He may be reserved or aloof around strangers.

Often, a Rottweiler will want to follow family members around the house, as the breed loves to be around people. They are very intelligent and enjoy training.

The description of temperament is, for me, one of the most important parts of the breed standard. A dog with so much size, strength, and power must have a good-natured temperament.

Parts of a Rottweiler

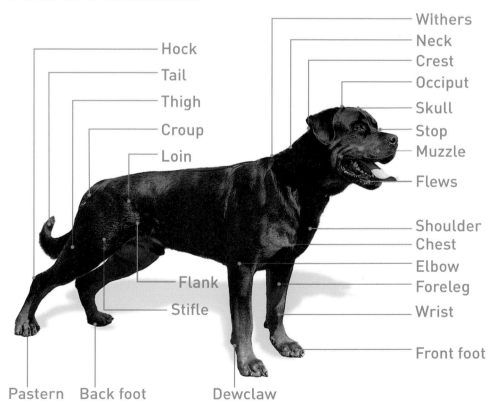

Withers
Neck
Crest
Occiput
Skull
Stop
Muzzle
Flews
Shoulder
Chest
Elbow
Foreleg
Wrist
Front foot

Hock
Tail
Thigh
Croup
Loin
Flank
Stifle

Pastern
Back foot
Dewclaw

Head and skull

The head is probably the main feature that distinguishes the Rottweiler from other breeds. The top of the skull should be broad between the ears and well muscled, giving the impression of power and substance.

Correct male heads should give the impression of overall masculinity. The female head may have slightly softer angles. Both sexes should have strong broad upper and lower jaws.

The top of the skull should have a slight arch from the stop (the spot where the muzzle meets the forehead) to the base of the skull, and from ear to ear, but not so arched as to give a domed effect. The skull should make up about 60 percent of the length from tip of nose to the back of the head, and the muzzle should make up the other 40 percent.

The skin should be smooth and not loose, although quite often you will see a few wrinkles on the top of a Rottweiler's head when he is attentive or alert.

Eyes

The eyes should be dark brown; anything lighter is considered undesirable. This is not so much a health consideration, as the eyes can work just as well regardless of the color, but it is an important trait. As the eye color gets lighter, it softens the appearance of the gaze, losing the fearlessness of the Rottweiler expression.

The shape of the eyes should be almond and not round, preferably set wide apart. They should be moderately deep-set, neither protruding nor receding. The eyelids should be tight fitting.

Ears

The ears should be the shape of an equilateral triangle and should sit close to the cheek, with the bottom tip lying flat to the cheek and not curling out. The ear set should increase the overall appearance of the size of the Rottweiler's head while remaining in proportion with it.

Mouth

The Rottweiler has strong, large teeth, which should meet in a scissors bite (the upper teeth slightly overlap the lower teeth evenly). The lips should always be black and firm—not flopping down like a Bloodhound's. Ideally, the gums should also be dark, although many Rottweilers do have pink gums.

Neck

To support and carry a Rottweiler's magnificent head, the neck needs to be of a fair length and very muscular. The breed standard specifies, "Powerful, well muscled, moderately long, slightly arched, and without loose skin."

Body

The front legs should be straight, muscular, with plenty of strength and substance, and the pasterns (the part between the foot and the leg) should slope slightly forward. The elbows should sit well under the body and not stick out or turn in. This will also determine the set of the feet, which should be straight, not standing at an angle.

The chest is broad and deep, with a straight back that is strong and not too long. The shoulders should be in proportion to the length of body. The loins should be short, strong and deep. The croup (area near the tail) should be in proportion to the body and very slightly sloping.

As it is the back end that powers this breed, the

muscles in the hindquarters should be well developed both in the upper and lower thigh. The stifles or knees should be fairly well angulated and not straight.

Feet

The feet should be round and compact with toes well arched, giving an overall neat look. The hind feet are somewhat longer than the front feet. The toenails should be short and black.

Tail

The tail should look as if it is an extension of the dog's topline. The Rottweiler is among a number of breeds of dogs whose tails were traditionally docked from birth. No one really knows why the Rottweiler's tail was originally docked, but there are a number of theories. Some say it may have been linked to taxes imposed on dogs. Working dogs may have been exempt from these taxes, and docking the tail could have been a way of proving he was a working dog. Others say they were docked to avoid damage from working alongside cattle.

Nowadays, the only reason for docking Rottweilers is for cosmetic purposes, and it is banned in many countries. However, docking is still allowed in the USA, and at dog shows, Rottweilers are usually shown with docked tails. If you prefer not to dock your dog's tail, you can still show him—and of course, he is still a great pet.

Gait/movement

Because the Rottweiler was initially bred to herd cattle, the overall movement should show off his strength and endurance. The best way to see a Rottweiler move is in the trot. He should be able to move efficiently and effortlessly, without showing any signs of lameness. When you watch him move, most of the power will come from the rear end, while the front legs stride out purposefully. His back should remain straight and balanced at all times.

Coat

The Rottweiler is a double-coated breed, which means that he has both a medium length topcoat and an undercoat. The topcoat is

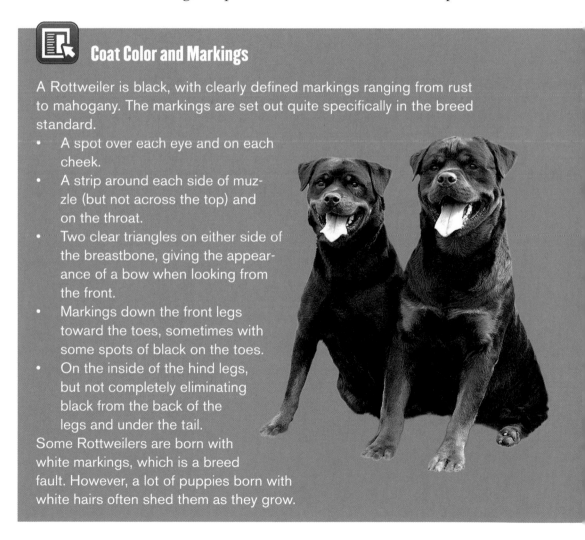

Coat Color and Markings

A Rottweiler is black, with clearly defined markings ranging from rust to mahogany. The markings are set out quite specifically in the breed standard.

- A spot over each eye and on each cheek.
- A strip around each side of muzzle (but not across the top) and on the throat.
- Two clear triangles on either side of the breastbone, giving the appearance of a bow when looking from the front.
- Markings down the front legs toward the toes, sometimes with some spots of black on the toes.
- On the inside of the hind legs, but not completely eliminating black from the back of the legs and under the tail.

Some Rottweilers are born with white markings, which is a breed fault. However, a lot of puppies born with white hairs often shed them as they grow.

straight, dense, and coarse to the touch. The undercoat should not show through the topcoat.

Size

Rottweilers should be slightly longer than they arc tall. They vary in size between dogs and bitches. According to the breed standard, the height at the withers (the top of the shoulder) should be 24 to 27 inches (61 to 69 cm) for dogs and 22 to 25 inches (56 to 63 cm) for bitches. This is only a guideline, as I have seen both dogs and bitches outside these measurements and, unless you want to show your dog, the size does not affect the overall health of your pet in any way.

Chapter 3

What Do You Want From Your Rottweiler?

The Rottweiler is one of the most versatile of all breeds and will excel in most fields. However, it is important that you decide what you want from your dog, so that she can live up to your expectations, and that you give her the lifestyle and training she needs.

Companion dog

Most Rottweiler puppies go to pet homes, and so the overriding considerations are health and temperament. Obviously, you want a healthy dog but equally important, you want a dog who is sound in temperament. This comes from her genetic make-up, so you need to check out her family background as thoroughly as possible—and the

rest is up to you. The Rottweiler has a superb temperament, but this is a breed that must have firm, fair, and consistent handling.

Working dog

Some owners know right from the start that they want to compete with their dog in one of the canine sports, such as obedience, tracking, working trials, schutzhund, or agility. The Rottweiler is a highly intelligent dog and, with the right training, most will do well in whatever discipline you choose.

Show dog

If you want to buy a puppy with the aim of showing her, you will need to research the breed standard to get a good idea of what qualities to look out for. If you let the breeder know, they will help you to choose the puppy with the most show potential.

Bear in mind that there is no guarantee a puppy with show potential will grow into a successful show dog. Youngsters can change considerably as they mature, so all you can go on is how the puppy looks at the time you are choosing her. It is also helpful if you see her close relatives, so you can form a picture of the type of Rottweiler a particular breeder produces.

Guard dog

The Rottweiler has natural guarding instincts when she matures, and this has proved to be a double-edged sword. Too many people have been attracted to the breed for the

wrong reasons, wanting to enhance their own image with a "macho" dog, or getting a Rottweiler in the belief that she will guard home and family without any training.

In fact, the Rottweiler's willingness to guard property is not guaranteed. This is not a breed that will flourish being chained up in a garden or used solely as a guard dog. If you want to protect your property, you would be better off investing in a more reliable alternative, such as a burglar alarm or a security system. A Rottweiler enjoys being with her family too much to thrive on this kind of life.

What your Rottweiler wants from you

Dog ownership is a life-long commitment, so the decision to bring a Rottweiler into your home should not be made lightly. Before getting a Rottweiler, you should research the breed so you know what you are taking on. Every person within the household should be committed to share in her upbringing and care.

Time

Your Rottweiler will be miserable—and possibly destructive—if she is left for long periods on her own. A dog should never be left for more than four hours at a stretch. If work commitments pose a problem, you will need to make alternative arrangements, such as hiring a dog sitter or a dog walker.

Training and socialization

The Rottweiler also needs an extensive program of socialization, so that she is able to cope calmly and confidently in all situations. That means introducing her to all kinds of people, places, and things. She also must be trained, or you will have a large, out-of-control dog.

Exercise

A Rottweiler needs an hour of exercise every day, and some kind of mental stimulation or training to exercise her brain as well as her body.

More to think about

Now that you've decided that the Rottweiler is the breed for you, you need to narrow your choice, so you know exactly what you are looking for. This will help in your search to find the ideal dog for your family.

Male or female?

The choice of male of female is a matter of personal preference, but there are some important considerations to bear in mind.

A male Rottweiler can grow up to 27 inches (69 cm) tall at the

withers (so that's not counting the neck and head!) and weigh up to 126 pounds (57 kg). Although very loving with his family, a male can be assertive with other dogs, and will pass through different stages of maturity with noticeable behavior changes.

Dogs 101: Rottweiler

If you have no plans to breed from your male Rottweiler, you would do well to consider neutering. Neutering has a number of health benefits, as well as making the dog easier to live with. Ask your veterinarian for further advice.

A female Rottweiler is usually smaller and lighter, but is still a big dog. Unlike the males, you will usually find that what you have from a young puppy is generally what you end up with in an adult. Generally, she will be more compliant than a male, and breeders will suggest that someone who has little or no experience with the breed should have a female, as they are much easier to handle.

If you take on a female, you will need to cope with her seasonal cycle, unless you have her spayed. Opinions vary as to when is the best time to do this, so ask your veterinarian for advice.

More than one?

More than one puppy in the house causes double the workload, requires double the time spent training each dog, and costs double the money in food, toys, and vet bills. You may also find that the two puppies bond so closely with each other that they may not care about the rest of the family. Alternatively, as they grow up, they may compete with each other, and this can cause problems with aggression.

If you want more than one, wait until your first dog is at least 18 months old, and fully trained, before taking on a new puppy.

Puppy or adult rescued dog?

It is a sad fact of life that many Rottweilers, through no fault of their own, end up in shelters and rescue organizations looking for a new forever home. You may want to weigh up the pros and cons between a puppy and an adult rescued dog.

If you take on a puppy, she comes with a relatively clean slate but brings a lot of upheaval to your home. You will have housetraining accidents, personal belongings may be chewed and destroyed, and, in the early days, you may have some sleepless nights.

The adult rescued dog will usually have basic training; many may just require some additional training to polish the edges. Adult dogs will usually be housetrained and are less likely to destroy things. The only downside is that you may not know their history. Some rescued dogs may require specialist training or may have a health problem that needs to be managed.

If, as a family, you decide that an adult dog is for you, there are a number of rescue organizations, some of which are dedicated specifically to the Rottweiler, who can help you find a dog who will suit your family and your situation.

Chapter 4

Finding Your Puppy

W here are you going to find a Rottweiler puppy who is sound, healthy, and typical of the breed? There are a couple of options, but some are far better than others.

Places to avoid

Many puppies are advertised on the Internet, and photos of Rottweiler puppies will look adorable. But not every adorable puppy grows into a healthy, well-adjusted adult. The Internet is a good source of information, but the recommended sites are those run by national kennel clubs, where you will also find advice about choosing a puppy and finding a reputable breeder. Breed clubs may also be able to put you in touch with breeders in your area.

Avoid a breeder who sells lots of different breeds of puppies. This could well indicate that the aim is to make as much money as possible rather than giving a lifetime's dedication to one special breed.

Avoid puppy farms, also known as puppy mills, at all costs. A puppy farm is a place where many puppies are bred and there are usually (but not always) many different breeds. They are run by unscrupulous breeders, who house adult dogs, often in appalling conditions, with no exercise or human interaction. Puppies are churned out with little or no consideration for the health of the mother dog or her babies. The puppies may be very young when they are taken from the mother, so will miss out on essential socialization, which will have a detrimental effect on their future development.

Dogs in pet stores come from puppy farms—even if the pet store tells you the dog is from a breeder. They mean a puppy farm breeder, not a responsible breeder.

Finding a responsible breeder

Responsible breeders raise their puppies at home and underfoot. They have one or, at the most, two litters at a time. They carefully study the pedigrees of the male and female before they arrange any breeding, with an eye toward breeding the healthiest, most temperamentally sound Rottweilers. Responsible breeders belong to a breed club and are involved in their breed.

Responsible breeders register their puppies with a well-established registry such as the American Kennel Club or the United Kennel Club. (Registration with a well-established kennel club is a guarantee that your Rottweiler is truly a Rottweiler, but it is not a guarantee of good health or temperament.) They are able to hand over registration documents at the time of sale. Their breeding dogs are permanently identified by microchip or DNA. They screen them for hereditary health problems, and can tell you exactly which screening tests their dogs have had and what the results were.

Responsible breeders socialize all their puppies in a home environment. They provide written advice on feeding, on-going training, socialization, parasite control, and vaccinations. They are available for phone calls after you buy their puppies, and will take a dog back at any time. They have a written contract of sale for each puppy that conforms to your state's laws.

Once you have a list of breeders, make several phone calls and do not be afraid to ask questions. A responsible breeder should find the time to answer all your queries, as well as giving you informa-

tion about the puppies they have bred. You should ask the breeder about the temperament of their lines and the socialization the puppies have received.

A responsible breeder will want to interview you, so be prepared to be questioned before you get the go-ahead to buy a puppy. The breeder will want to know about your home and family set-up, and if you plan to get involved in showing or any of the dog sports. Do not be intimidated by such breeders; they want what is best for the breed and for their dogs.

Health issues

Like all breeds, the Rottweiler does have some inherited health issues, so the first question you should ask the breeder is if the dam

(mother) and sire (father) have had the relevant health checks. For the Rottweiler, this should include tests for hip dysplasia and elbow dysplasia; eye testing is a bonus.

Puppy watching

Rottweiler puppies are like little woolly teddy bears and are totally irresistible. However, you are only going to take one puppy home with you, so how do you choose?

The best time to visit is when the puppies are about five weeks old, because they are mobile and their characters will be forming. You should expect to visit the puppies at least twice before taking your puppy home.

The puppies should appear happy and healthy, with bright eyes showing no discharge, and healthy, shiny coats without signs of baldness or sores on the skin. It is important to see the mother with her puppies, as this will give you some idea of the temperament they are likely to inherit.

Cute Rottweiler puppies

The mother should be friendly and you should ask to interact with her, even if only to make a fuss over her. If the breeder is reluctant to let you do this, there may be an issue with temperament, so walk away! Although the male's genes contribute to the overall temperament of the puppies, the mother's close contact and influence plays a great part in the development of the puppies' character.

Sometimes the breeder will own the father, although this is rare—quite often the male is from another kennel and from different bloodlines. However, you should be able to see photos of the stud dog, and check out his pedigree, his show record, and make sure he has been health tested.

The right choice

The puppies should approach you, sniff, and then act confident around you. Remember that puppies do chew and bite, so seeing this behavior does not mean they are going to be aggressive.

Spend some time with the puppies and only pick one after you decide you are truly happy with the way the puppies act and look. Remember that all puppies are cute, and it is often our instinct to rescue ill-looking or unhappy-looking puppies. This is done at a potentially high cost to you at a later date. If you have any concerns about health, ask your veterinarian to come and visit the puppies. If you cannot arrange this, ask the breeder if they are prepared to offer you a full refund within 48 hours of taking the puppy, and get the puppy checked by your vet when you first take her home.

Show puppy

If you have plans to show your Rottweiler, the breeder will help you pick out a puppy who has the correct conformation, movement, and markings at this early stage.

Ideally, you want a solid puppy who has good substance, along with a strong head with a short, broad muzzle. The eyes should be dark, as should the pigment around the mouth. The puppy should have good, straight front legs when standing alert. The colors should be black and a rich mahogany, without any trace of white in the coat. The coat itself should be short and not wavy. Chances are, if the parents are from good show stock, the puppies are likely to inherit the correct conformation.

Chapter 5

A Rottweiler- Friendly Home

t will soon be time to bring your Rottweiler puppy home. But before you do this, make sure you're ready. There is much to plan and consider—and buy!—before your dog comes home.

House rules

First off, agree on all the ground rules before the puppy comes into your home, and make sure the whole family sticks to the same rules. A puppy needs consistent handling by everyone or he will very quickly become confused.

Rottweilers are very much people dogs. They like to follow their owners around the house and will often just lie down in the room you happen to be in. If, for whatever reason, you do not want your dog to do this, he must be taught right from the start that some rooms are off-limits. This is easily done by using baby gates (also known as puppy gates) to block off restricted areas.

Safety at home

Check your home to ensure that your little pup will be safe. All puppies chew, so any wires that are accessible should be secured, or the area needs to be one where your puppy is not allowed to access. Cleaning materials and detergents should be shut away in cabinets as they are potentially lethal if ingested by an inquisitive puppy. Make sure that children's toys are not left around, as these can be harmful to a puppy, who likes to test everything with his mouth. The same goes for smaller articles of clothing and any knickknacks at puppy head height.

In the yard

The yard must be surrounded by secure fencing that should be

at least 6 feet (1.8 m) high. Walk the perimeter of the fence to check for any holes your puppy can get through or under. Being naturally curious animals, pups will take these escape routes to explore.

If you have plants in your garden and you are fond of them, you will need to fence off an area to prevent your puppy from getting to them. Rottweilers are great diggers and will have endless fun ripping up your prize perennials and burying toys and bones in their place. Also watch out for plants that are poisonous to dogs; you can find a full list on the website of the ASPCA (www.aspca.org).

Finding a veterinarian

Do this before you bring your dog home, so you have a vet to call if there is a problem. Consult friends who own dogs. Breed clubs can also provide lists of recommended vets, including, in some cases, veterinarians with special knowledge of Rottweilers.

Shopping for your Rottweiler

It's best to buy what you need before you bring your dog home. You'll have enough to do with a new dog in the house! If you choose wisely, the equipment will last for many years.

Sleeping quarters

Rottweiler puppies can be very destructive, and may shred a fabric bed. A plastic bed that is lined with washable (and replaceable) synthetic fleece-style bedding is ideal.

I highly recommend all dog owners buy a crate and train your puppy to sleep in it from the first day. The crate should be large enough to house an adult Rottweiler stretched out, but initially it should be set up so that the bed is placed in one half and the other half is lined with newspaper to provide a toilet area. Arrange a sheet or blanket across the top of the crate to make it more den-like.

Crate training can begin from day one. Start by feeding your dog or puppy all his meals in his crate, and encourage him to sleep in there with the door open. It is essential that he never considers being put in his crate as a punishment. This has to be an area where he feels safe and secure.

Bowls

Your new puppy will need a bowl for both his food and another one for his water. The safest type is made of stainless steel, which is easy to clean and indestructible. Make sure the bowl is big enough for the formidable head of an adult Rottweiler.

Collar and leash

Your puppy will grow at an alarming rate, and the initial puppy collar and leash set will probably only last a few weeks. The collar should fit snugly against your dog's neck; you should be able to fit two fingers between the collar and his neck.

As your puppy grows, you will need to buy a bigger, slightly wider collar; one that is about an inch (2.5 cm) wide is perfectly sufficient. Get a flat collar with a buckle (not a snap fastener, as these can come apart at a crucial moment). Start with nylon, and graduate to

leather when your dog is full-grown.

The leash should allow your dog to walk comfortably at your side—about 3 feet (1 meter) long is ideal—and it should be made of a good-quality leather or nylon.

Identification

When your Rottweiler is out in public places, he needs to have some form of ID. Pet supply stores and some veterinary practices sell dog tags and will engrave them with your contact details. Or you can get contact details embroidered on to the collar. However, permanent ID, such as microchipping, is a good idea. A microchip is a tiny glass-encased chip that is inserted under the skin with a needle. It can be done on very young puppies, and feels about the same as an injection.

Toys

Rottweilers like nothing more than to play and interact with their owners. When choosing toys for your puppy or adult dog, look for things that are tough and durable.

A ball is great fun, but make sure it is one with a rope attached, and always check regularly for damage. Rottweilers also like soft toys, but be careful when choosing these types of toys, as they can be ripped apart in no time, and if the dog swallows any of the stuffing, it can cause problems.

Tug toys are also very good for Rottweilers, as this encourages play and interaction with you, thus strengthening the bond between you. However, this type of game is best avoided with a young puppy, especially during the teething stages, as it could cause tooth pain.

If you are going out and want to leave your Rottweiler with something to amuse himself, a Kong (a hollow, rubber, cone-shaped toy, which can be filled with something tasty) or other type of food toy is probably one of the best things to keep him occupied. These can be bought in most pet supply stores or online.

Grooming gear

Initially, all you need is a soft brush so your puppy gets used to being groomed. This can be replaced with a rubber brush when the adult coat comes in.

Settling in

The big day has finally arrived and it is time to go get your puppy. Ask the breeder if you can arrive in the morning, to allow your puppy time to settle in once he is home. If possible, ask for a piece of bedding with a familiar smell that you can take home with you, as this will help make the transition less stressful.

When your puppy arrives in his new home, try to keep the environment as quiet as possible. Avoid having too many people crowding him—your friends can come and meet your new Rottweiler another day, after he has settled in. Let your puppy explore the areas of the house and yard that will be his environment. Although it's tempting, try not to lavish too much attention on your puppy too quickly; this is a scary situation for him and he needs time to get used to both the environment and his new family.

Meeting the family

Rottweilers and children can live together harmoniously as long as everyone understands the rules. It is important to remember that a puppy is not a toy for your children and should not be carried around like a doll or a teddy bear. Puppies' bones are soft and a child can easily damage joints by accidentally dropping, or falling on, a pup.

All puppies test with their teeth, and although undesirable, nipping is perfectly natural behavior. Littermates bite one another and play rough, and your puppy will probably think his new human family will continue these games. Children should learn that when the puppy does nip, they should say "ouch" and then walk away, telling the puppy in a language he understands that this is not the way to behave.

Involve all family members with the day-to-day care of your puppy; this will foster deep bonds with the whole family, as opposed to just one person. Encourage the children to train and reward the puppy, teaching him to follow their cues as he would an adult's.

The animal family

I have always introduced my dogs to a new puppy before the puppy actually comes home. Dogs learn a lot through smell, so make sure that when you visit your puppy at the breeder, he gets a chance to smell the other animals on you. Cuddle him to you throughout the visit and, when you go home, allow your dogs at home to have a good sniff of you and your clothing while you make a gentle fuss of them. If you can do this more than once, all the better.

On the day you bring the puppy home, sit with him on your lap and let your other dog have a sniff and satisfy his curiosity, calmly stroking both dogs. The most important thing is not to discipline the older dog, but to encourage him to be gentle around the puppy.

Take care at mealtimes, and prevent your puppy from trying to take food from your older dog—or vice versa. The safest is to feed both dogs separately. I recommend that all interactions between your dog and your new puppy be supervised until they have established a good relationship.

If you are bringing home an adult dog, introductions should be on neutral ground on a leash, before you bring the newest member of the family home. Most reputable rescue organizations will insist on this to ensure your Rottweiler has a smooth transition into his new home.

Meeting a cat should be supervised in a similar way, but do not allow your puppy to be rough with her. Most cats are more than capable of looking after themselves, but take care at the first meeting to prevent any unwanted animosity, as this will only progress as the puppy grows. Given time and supervision, there is no reason why a Rottweiler cannot live very happily with a cat.

Rottweilers have quite a high prey drive, and small animals such as hamsters and rabbits could quite easily become prey for your puppy. Again, allowing the puppy to sniff the small animal, making himself familiar with it, will help, but care must be taken at all times to ensure that the small animal is never left out of a secure cage or pen when your Rottweiler is around. Instinct is a very hard thing for him to battle, so you need to take care that your puppy does not get into the habit of chasing smaller animals.

Feeding

Most breeders will provide diet instructions for you to follow, and usually will give you a small bag of food to take home with you. It is important to follow this diet for the first few weeks, as this will help the settling-in period to go smoothly.

If you want to change your pup's dog food, do it gradually by mixing some of the new food with his old diet and then slowly increasing the amount of the new food and decreasing the old. Watch carefully for any changes in your dog's behavior and toileting, as the new food may not be suitable and you might have to rethink his diet.

The first night

Your puppy will have spent the first weeks of his life either with his mother or curled up with his siblings. He is then taken from everything he knows as familiar and is often lavished with attention by his new family for several hours. Then comes bedtime. He is placed in his crate, all the lights are switched off, and he is abandoned—at least, that is how he feels. This is why puppies howl at night—not always from distress, as we often interpret, but because howling is an effective way for a dog to call to his canine family.

I prefer to have the crate in my bedroom at night so the puppy is always with his human family. After the first few nights you can start to move the crate out of the bedroom and to wherever it will be permanently (which could remain your bedroom). I have followed this routine with most of my dogs, and I have never had a problem with sleepless nights. Having the pup in my room means I am also aware of when the puppy needs to toilet, and have thus been able to take him outside, making housetraining that much quicker.

If you decide against this, make sure you do not make a big fuss over your puppy when you leave him. Leave a couple of teddy bears in his bed to represent other puppies, and leave a radio playing quietly in his room. Make sure the radio is tuned into talking rather than music, as this will be more soothing to a puppy.

If he howls in the night, the best thing is to ignore him. This could go on for some time and carry on for several nights, so if you are taking this route, it may be a good idea to warn your neighbors. Going in to comfort a puppy who howls is just rewarding him for this behavior, and will encourage him to continue to howl.

Housetraining

The key to housetraining your puppy is to be vigilant and consistent, so that you establish a routine your puppy understands. The fewer mistakes he makes, the sooner he will learn to be clean in the house.

The breeder may have started the process of housetraining by teaching the puppies to relieve themselves on newspaper, or even in a litterbox or outside. Puppies have a natural desire to keep the nest or bed area clean and go elsewhere for toileting.

When your puppy arrives in his new home, you can continue this

 Rescued Dogs

Settling an adult, rescued dog into your home is very similar to a puppy, and you will need to have made the same preparations for his homecoming. As with a puppy, an adult dog will need you to be consistent, so start as you mean to go on.

There is often a honeymoon period when you first bring home a rescued dog, where he will be on his best behavior for the first few weeks. It is after these first couple of weeks that the true nature of the dog will show, so be prepared for subtle changes in his behavior. Enroll with a reputable training school so that any problems can be quickly and easily dealt with, and you can brush up his training. Above all, remember that a rescued dog ceases to be a rescued dog the moment he enters his forever home, and should be treated like any other family member.

process by moving the paper nearer and nearer to the back door and eventually out to the yard or the sidewalk. However, you may prefer to cut out this interim phase and establish a routine of taking your puppy outside at regular intervals.

A small puppy will need to relieve himself frequently. The best plan is to take him out at the following times:

- First thing in the morning
- After mealtimes
- After waking up from a nap
- After a play session
- Last thing at night

Do not leave more than two-hour gaps between trips outside; hourly outings are ideal if you can manage them.

It helps if you have a designated toileting area in the yard or outside in the street, so your puppy will associate it with relieving himself. When your puppy performs, give him lots of praise and, maybe, a treat, so he knows how pleased you are with him. When he understands what is required, you can use a verbal cue, such as "Be clean," which will be useful for getting a quicker response, and you can also use it when you are away from home.

Do not rush back into the house as soon as your puppy has relieved himself, because then he might start to employ delaying tactics. Spend a few minutes playing with pup before heading indoors.

When accidents happen

If you catch your puppy soiling in the house, try clapping your hands to startle him and, hopefully, interrupt his toilet. Carry him outside and stay with him. Eventually he will need to finish what he started in the house, and when he does, praise and reward him.

Never scold your puppy for accidents in the house, as all this will do is cause anxieties about toileting. He may worry about relieving himself in front of you, and will find secret places to go in the house instead. If your puppy has an accident, remember to use an enzymatic cleaner designed for pet urine, to discourage him for using that spot again.

Choosing a diet

There is a wide variety of dog food available, and the choice can be bewildering. The aim is to find a diet that will suit your dog, and is convenient for you to buy and feed. A complete diet is scientifically manufactured to cater to all your dog's nutritional needs and should not be supplemented. Many manufacturers produce diets for different life stages, such as puppy, adult, veteran, or for nursing bitches, and there are some that are designed for particular breeds.

When choosing a dog food, it is important to study the additives and protein content. I am often faced with hyperactive puppies at my training school, possibly because of foods that are either too high in protein or have too many additives. Check the ingredients, as they are listed in order of greatest quantity.

Ideally, your Rottweiler should be on a diet that is mainly meat and backed with a good source of grain, such as rice or oats. Look for foods that are free of wheat and dairy products, as these are foods often associated with allergies in dogs.

Be aware of price, as a cheap dog food could be lower in quality, and it is essential that your Rottweiler puppy has a good-quality diet to encourage healthy growth.

Dry food

Most dry foods, or kibble, are scientifically formulated to meet all your dog's nutritional needs. There are many brands of kibble available, and most offer life-stage foods, such as puppy, adult, and senior. There are also special diets for pregnant bitches, working dogs, and prescription diets for weight control, and other health-related conditions.

Which kibble is best? This is a difficult question, but the best plan is to seek advice from your puppy's breeder or your veterinarian.

Kibble can be fed on its own, or along with other types of food. It is best fed in a puzzle toy—a toy dogs must manipulate in some way to get the food out. No dog is too young—or too old!—to start eating kibble from a puzzle toy.

Canned food

Canned food contains a lot more water than kibble. Some canned foods—although certainly not all—will have fewer carbohydrates than kibble. Read the label carefully so you are aware of the ingredients and, remember, what you put in will affect what comes out.

Canned food can be all or part of your dog's diet. Even if it is only a part, the label should say the diet is complete and balanced for your dog.

Natural diets

Raw diets may come fresh or frozen or freeze-dried, or you might choose to prepare your dog's diet yourself. They typ-

Choosing dog food

ically contain raw meat, bones, organ meats, fat, vegetables, and sometimes, some cooked grains. Proponents of raw diets believe they are providing the dog with a food that is very close to the natural diet if she would eat in the wild.

If you're buying a raw diet, look for a statement on the label that says it's complete and balanced. If you want to prepare the diet yourself, work with a veterinary nutritionist to formulate a healthy diet for your dog. There are a lot of raw diet recipes on the Internet, but recent research has found that the majority of them do not offer complete and balanced nutrition.

A feeding schedule

At first Rottweiler puppies should be fed four times a day. You can cut down to three times when they are about four months old, and then down to twice daily from around six months. As the dog grows, so does the stomach, so you can increase each meal to meet this daily feeding requirement.

I would never feed a Rottweiler less often than twice daily, as feeding too much in one sitting can cause an often-fatal condition called gastric torsion, where gases build up in the stomach, causing it to twist. For the same reason, avoid exercise and play with your Rottweiler for approximately two hours before and after each meal, to allow the food to settle.

A Rottweiler should not be fat at any time in his life, as carrying too much weight could prove harmful. You should be able to feel the dog's ribs when you run your hands along his sides, but they should not be visible when your dog is standing relaxed.

Mealtimes

Your puppy's feeding times will be initially guided by the breeder, and it is important that you stick to these times as much as possible to ease the settling-in process. When you begin reducing the number of meals, the times can be adjusted to better suit your lifestyle. Dogs are creatures of habit and will soon become used to eating at set times.

I always vary the times of meals so my dogs are not expecting dinner at a certain time, mainly because I am unable to feed my dogs every day at exactly the same time.

Fresh drinking water should be available to your dog at all times and never withheld for any reason.

Ideal weight

The average weight for the adult Rottweiler is 110 pounds (50 kg) for a male and 93 pounds (42 kg) for a female—although this will certainly vary with the size of the dog. That weight does not need to be achieved by the time the puppy is six months old. However, a puppy needs the correct amount of food so that he can develop strong, healthy bones. An underfed Rottweiler can develop food aggression issues simply because he is hungry.

Dog food manufacturers put a daily feeding guide on their label. You can follow those guidelines, as long as you are checking that your puppy is not looking too fat or too thin. If you are unsure at any time, ask your vet for advice. Getting it right at this stage is crucial, as it will determine how your puppy develops.

Bones and chews

Rottweilers love to chew, and you can give them something long lasting, such as a large, rawhide chew, to enjoy for a couple of hours. Never leave your dog with this kind of treat, as I have heard of dogs choking on large pieces that they have tried to swallow whole. Also avoid rawhide chews that have knots at either end, as your dog can bite off and swallow the knots, which may get stuck in his throat or anywhere along his digestive system.

A raw meat bone from the butcher is another great treat for your dog, but make sure it is a knucklebone so he will not break his teeth.

Chapter 6

Caring for Your Rottweiler

The Rottweiler is an easy breed to care for, but you should set time aside every week to check him over and keep him well-groomed and clean. Care also includes physical and mental exercise for your dog throughout his life.

Grooming

As soon as your puppy has settled into his new home, get him accustomed to grooming. Use a pin brush to work through his coat, and give him lots of praise and treats when he cooperates. When you are grooming, check for any lumps or bumps and for fleas or ticks that may be making a home on your dog. If you notice anything out of the ordinary, it is best to get it checked by your vet.

The adult Rottweiler has a topcoat and an undercoat, and will shed most heavily at the change of seasons—use an undercoat rake to cut down on hair around the house.

Bathing

Excessive bathing can strip your dog's coat of its natural oils. I bathe my dogs twice a year at the most. This can be a daunting task, and, if finances permit, I suggest taking him to a groomer, as it will have the facilities to bathe and groom your dog, and the experience to do this with minimum stress to the animal.

If your dog has rolled in something unpleasant—which all dogs like to do—apply diluted lemon juice on the affected area, which will remove the smell, and, once dry, rinse with warm water. This can take the place of a full bath.

Rottweiler Care Tips

The shortcoated Rottweiler needs little more than a weekly brushing.

You can clean your Rottweiler's ears with a soft, damp wipe, but do not probe into the ear canal.

Make sure you trim only the tip of the nail.

Regular tooth brushing will help prevent tartar build-up.

Regular checks

From an early age, your Rottweiler should be accustomed to being examined all over, because you will need to be able to do this throughout his life. Start out by using treats; feed your puppy with one hand while running your other hand over his body and checking his ears, teeth, and feet.

Teeth

Rottweiler puppies should have 28 temporary teeth that erupt at about three to four weeks old. They will eventually have 42 permanent adult teeth that begin to emerge at about three to four months of age. When your Rottweiler is getting his adult teeth, his gums and mouth will be tender and it is best to avoid handling his mouth too much at this time.

When the adult teeth are in place, it is important to look after them. There are chews on the market designed to loosen plaque and help keep your dog's teeth clean, but you'll also need to brush his teeth once or twice a week, using a soft toothbrush and dog toothpaste. Only use toothpaste that is designed for dogs, as human toothpaste can be harmful if swallowed.

Ears

Check your Rottweiler's ears every month, and if they are dirty you can use an ear-cleaning solution that you can buy from your vet. Soak a cotton ball with the solution and wipe around the inside of the ear. Never go deeper into the ear than your first finger joint.

Nails

It is important to cut your Rottweiler's nails every two or three weeks. Nails that are allowed to grow too long will force your dog's toes to splay and could result in lameness.

Rottweilers tend to have sensitive feet, so you will need to hold his feet, gently feeling between his toes, while feeding him treats to make him believe he is having a good experience. Start this right from the beginning, so your puppy gets used to it.

Because a Rottweiler's nails are black, they are not easy to trim, because you are not able to see the quick (the bundle of nerves and blood vessels). If you do cut through the quick, it will hurt, and, most importantly, he will remember this experience and may not be so keen to allow you to trim his nails in the future.

The safest way to trim nails is to hold your dog's foot securely and clip just under the curve of the nail, removing tiny pieces at a time. Do not forget the dewclaws, which are located farther up your Rottweiler's front legs.

Exercising your Rottweiler

The Rottweiler is a working dog and is not happy to just laze around the house. He needs daily exercise and training to keep his mind and body stimulated and ensure he remains a stable and pleasant companion.

Daily exercise will help to keep your Rottweiler at the correct weight and will also help prevent unwanted behavior, such as chewing and digging, brought on by boredom. Daily walks in a busy environment are an ideal way to socialize your Rottweiler and will also help deepen the bond between you.

While your puppy is growing, jumping must be limited, as he could damage his developing joints. For the same reason, you should prevent your puppy from jumping in and out of the car, and running up and down stairs.

Until your Rottweiler puppy is fully grown, walking should be restricted to no more than two 20-minute walks each day. Make the most of these outings by exposing your pup to many different environments.

Once fully grown, you will need to walk your Rottweiler for about an hour each day. Until you are sure your dog will come back

to you every time you call him, he should not be let off his leash in an unfenced area.

Rottweilers love water and will enjoy an outing to the beach, river, or lake where they can swim and play in the water. Do be careful of currents and tides, and do not exhaust your dog by endlessly throwing a ball into the water when he is not used to it.

Playing with your Rottweiler

Play not only provides an excellent source of exercise but also strengthens the bond between dog and owner. Rottweilers like nothing more than a game of tug or to have a ball thrown for them to chase.

Wrestling Games

Never play wrestling games with your Rottweiler, because it can rapidly get out of hand. As your puppy's strength grows, he is going to want to play fight to see who is stronger. Even if you win the match, he will learn that this type of play is acceptable—which it is not, at any time.

Your Rottweiler is growing into a very large, strong dog. He will not know the difference between wrestling with you or a much smaller, older, or younger member of the family. Having an adult Rottweiler leaping on someone for a rough and tumble is definitely a no-no.

Stick to fetch and tug and other games that do not involve him putting his mouth or paws on your body.

Tug-of-war games should be gentle (his teeth are changing), and your puppy should be taught that there are rules to the game , such as letting go when asked and being careful not to catch your hands.

Use a food reward to offer as a swap, so your dog is always happy to give you his toy, and make sure as soon as he has done this, the game continues either by throwing the ball again or restarting the tug game. He will learn from this not to become toy aggressive, as it is more fun to share.

The older Rottweiler

As your Rottweiler reaches his twilight years, you will find that he requires less exercise. From about the age of seven, his muscle tone will be harder to maintain and he will start developing gray hairs around the muzzle. He will seem content to spend more time sleeping and less time playing.

An older Rottweiler may develop arthritis in his later years and you may notice that he seems stiff when getting up from his bed. If you can keep his joints supple with regular gentle exercise, this will

help. Swimming is especially good for older dogs, as long as they do not get chilled. It is also advisable to watch his weight to keep extra pressure off stiff or aching joints. Incontinence is something older dogs may face, but your vet can usually prescribe medication for this. Your Rottweiler may lose some hearing or his sight may diminish. As with humans, you need to tolerate these changes with patience and respect. If your Rottweiler starts to lose his sight, try to keep furniture in the same place so you don't confuse him.

Letting go

It is a sad fact of life that only a small number of dogs die in their sleep. That means it is likely that at some point you will have to make the difficult decision to say good-bye to your beloved Rottweiler. This is the one time when you cannot be selfish and must think only of his needs. Your dog will usually tell you when the time has come, by showing an unwillingness to eat, walk, or leave his bed. Looking into his eyes, you will see that the sparkle has gone. You must let him go with his dignity.

If you do not want to face the ordeal of going to the vet clinic, a vet will come to your home. It is the very last thing you will do for your companion, so you must stay with him, reassuring him that all is well until the very end. It is the least you can do to repay him for all the fun and enjoyment he has given you over the years.

Given time, you will be able to look back with fondness on the times you shared, and laugh at some of the antics you both got up to. I would never give up the pleasure of owning a Rottweiler, because the good memories that are created far outweigh the grief of losing your dog.

Although you can never replace a beloved pet, you can replace the relationship and fun times you had with him, so maybe in time you can consider getting another dog to share your life with.

Chapter 7

Understanding and Training Your Rottweiler

Every dog is an individual and, over a period of time, you will reach a true understanding with your Rottweiler. You will know when she is in high spirits, when she feels worried, or when she is simply clowning around. You will discover all this by observation, but it will help if you have some knowledge of the developmental stages your Rottweiler is going through, as this will help you raise her right and train her well.

Stages of development

Dogs can learn throughout their lives, but the period from when they are about seven weeks to sixteen weeks is an optimum time, because they will absorb information very quickly. This also means

you must ensure that their experiences during this time are positive, because as easily as they learn the behaviors you want, they can also learn behaviors you don't want. Lots of changes occur as dogs mature, and you will notice that the stages described here overlap.

Birth to six weeks

It is important for your puppy to remain with her mother and siblings through this phase, as she begins to develop canine social skills and establish relationships with her littermates and with adult dogs—starting with her mother. Mom will teach her the first social skills, such as play and bite inhibition. Leaving her mother too early (before seven weeks) can have a life-long effect on her behavior with other dogs.

During this phase a puppy begins to form social relationships with other animals and humans, and to habituate to her environment. Throughout this phase, a good breeder will introduce your puppy to household sounds, smells, and objects, and contact with a variety of people.

Seven to 16 weeks

This time includes periods where the puppy will continue to build social relationships with other dogs, other animals, and humans. She will also need to be exposed to as many of the everyday environments as possible that she will encounter later as an adult dog. There is no consensus on the best time to let a puppy go to her new home, but most agree that she should be at least eight weeks old.

Although she will have a short attention span, it is during this time that your puppy will experience her most rapid learning, and what is taught in this period will remain with her for life. It is therefore the most vital time to introduce a puppy to different environments and people and to make sure that she has plenty of positive experiences. Even though she will not have received her final vaccinations until around 12 weeks, it is still essential to take her out to different places. If necessary, carry your puppy in your arms and allow people to handle and make a fuss over her. Introduce her to the sounds of busy roads and every day household noises.

From approximately eight to 11 weeks, your puppy will also experience her first fear period. During socialization it is important to make sure that she does not have any frightening or painful experiences, as puppies of this age generalize their experiences and can become timid and fearful. Should she display any signs of fear or stress during this time, the best thing is to remove her quietly from what is

scaring her. Do not make a big fuss, as this may reinforce her fears.

From about 10 to 16 weeks, your puppy will begin to work out her place in your household, and she may begin to test her position within the family. It is vital at this time that ground rules have been put in place and all the family is being consistent about them. For example, it is no good if one person allows the puppy on the sofa when another person does not. It is said that what you see at 16 weeks, without any training, is more or less what your dog will be like in her adult life. This is why training at this age is vital, so any unwanted behavior can be prevented.

Toward the end of this period, your puppy will begin losing her baby teeth, and mouthing family members can be a problem. Bite inhibition will have been started by the mother and littermates, but this needs to be continued by your family—which has replaced her canine family. Never smack your puppy for mouthing, just calmly say either "no" or "ouch" and walk away. If she persists, quietly put her in her crate for a few minutes to calm down.

Four to eight months

During this time, your dog could show a reluctance to please you and you may well see her test her limits more and more. It is very important to begin training and socialization before this time. You need to remain firm, fair, and above all consistent in your training. The adolescent Rottweiler is no different from the average teenage child; as long as the rules are clear, she will accept them with a minimum of fuss.

You can avoid problems with chewing by introducing safe chew toys, such as Kongs and Nylabones, and keeping temptations such as shoes put away.

Six to 14 months

From about six months to nine months, the Rottweiler starts to become sexually mature and you may see differences in the behavior of your dog, especially with males who may start to urine mark and mount more frequently. They may also become growly with other male dogs. This is often a stage they will pass through, but it is important that training and socialization continues. Some people suggest ignoring the inter-dog aggression, but it is best that the dogs learn that it is unacceptable with a firm "no" or "leave it" cue. Increased territoriality can occur, and some dogs can become more assertive when their owners control them. Again, it is very important that socialization and training continue and that household rules remain clear and consistent.

Female dogs generally have their first season between six months to one year of age, and you may see changes in scent marking behavior and solicitation of male attention.

The changes in hormones mean that your young dog may experience a second fear imprint period. This period is where your dog could show fear of something new or even something she is familiar with. If she reacts this way, the best thing is to play down the whole situation. Distract her from the object of her fear as best you can, or even better, remove her from it. Again it is important not to fuss and reassure your dog too much, as this will only reinforce her fear. Positive training during this period usually helps boost her confidence.

One to four years

Rottweilers are sexually mature by the time they are about one year old, often earlier. However, they continue to mature mentally and physically for some time after this. This period of social maturity brings together the dog's increasing social skills, size, and experience. There can be an increase in assertive behavior over unfamiliar dogs, and also toward people and dogs within their canine and human families, so training must continue into adulthood. It is vital at this stage that you remain firm but fair with your dog.

Training guidelines

The Rottweiler, although sometimes strong-willed, is very keen to learn and eager to please. Training will provide hours of pleasure for both you and your dog. To get the best results, it is important to think in advance about what you want to achieve, and the best ways to reach your goals.

How dogs learn

Dogs learn by trying out a behavior and evaluating its consequence, be it positive or negative. For example, when teaching your Rottweiler to come to you in the park, if she receives praise and some one-on-one play for coming to you, she is more likely to come every time she is called. If you snap on her leash and take her home, she is less likely to come the next time you call.

Rottweilers respond best to positive consequences—that is, rewards. These could be food or anything else your dog likes. An example of negative training would be to force your dog into a sit position if she will not sit when asked, or to smack her on the nose for mouthing. Negative training or punishment can lead to your Rottweiler becoming aggressive or fearful of you, and will not help in building a bond between dog and owner.

Giving rewards

Rewarding with treats is a very good way to teach a Rottweiler, as they all love food. When choosing a treat, remember what it is called—a treat. Working for regular kibble, which your dog gets at mealtimes for free, is hardly worth her while. But if you offer something really tasty, such as cheese, liver, or sausage, it will be a different story and you will have a willing pupil on your hands.

The key to successful dog training is making yourself so interesting that your dog will always want to respond to your cues, because she has learned that this produces something she loves.

Some Rottweilers also like to play, and if you can reward your dog with a satisfying game of tug or ball, this can help strengthen the bond between you.

First lessons

It is important, as a family unit, to decide what specific verbal cues you are going to give to the exercises you teach your Rottweiler, and to stick to them. You should only use a cue once, in a way that your dog will easily understand. Repeating cues over and over can become confusing for your dog.

Wearing a collar

Make sure your puppy is used to wearing his collar and leash around the house before taking her out. The first few times she's wearing her collar, she will stop and scratch and it will feel alien to her. If you attach a leash too soon, there is a good chance she will fight it and her first experience of going out will be marred by having a negative experience with both the collar and the leash.

Watch me

This cue is very useful, as it provides a great way to get your dog's attention. "Watch me" cue focuses your dog on making eye contact with you in a nonthreatening way. It is a great cue to use if you need to distract your dog at any time.

• Position your dog so that she is sitting in front of you, on a leash if necessary. Have a treat in your hand.

• Bring the treat from your dog's nose to your eyes, and, when she follows the food and her eyes meets yours, praise and reward.

• Repeat this process a few times each day before gradually removing the lure of the treat and adding the cue "watch me" as her eyes meet yours.

Walking on a leash

The key to teaching this exercise is patience. Walking your dog should be a pleasurable and stress-free experience. Having an adult Rottweiler towing you to the park is neither, and can also be dangerous.

• Begin training this exercise when your puppy is small by holding a treat or a toy in the hand that she is walking by. Hold the leash in the other hand so that it hangs across the front of you.

• Before you set off, make sure you have her attention; using the "watch me" cue works very well here. Then cue "heel" or "walk" and set off. Because she is watching you, she will have stayed by your side, so, after a couple of paces, praise and reward. Continue doing this, building up the number of paces in between each reward.

• As your Rottweiler grows in size, she may well begin to pull on a leash to get to where she wants to go even faster. Remain calm and just stop altogether until she makes eye contact with you—usually when she wants to know why you have stopped!

• When she responds, ask her to come close and start the exercise again. She will soon learn that pulling will not get her where she wants to be any quicker.

Remember to praise and reward when your dog is walking nicely to heel. We are often guilty of nagging when things go wrong and keeping quiet when the dog is responding correctly. She will never learn this way!

Socialization

The breeder will have started socializing the puppies, and this is a process you will need to continue intensively for the next 12 months—and, indeed, throughout your Rottweiler's life.

To begin with, your puppy needs to get used to her home environment and meet a variety of different people. When she has completed her vaccinations, you can venture into the outside world. Start off in quiet areas and then proceed to busier environments as your Rottweiler gains in confidence.

If your puppy seems anxious, do not pander to her or she will begin to think there really is something to worry about. Encourage her in a calm, businesslike manner, and she will realize there is nothing to be frightened of and will learn to cope in a variety of different situations.

It is also important to socialize your Rottweiler with other dogs of sound temperament, so that she learns the skills of canine communication. If dogs learn how to read each other's body language, it is much easier to avoid conflict. This is particularly important with the Rottweiler, who can be assertive with other dogs.

Come when called

This exercise should always be taught in a fun manner with a maximum reward offered at the end. Without a solid recall, you should not let your Rottweiler off her leash in unfenced areas.

Begin in the home from the time your puppy comes to live with you.

• Kneel on the floor so you are at your puppy's level and call her name, followed by your recall cue. Most people use the word "come." It is up to you what cue you use, as long as you stick to the same one. You can also clap your hands to make yourself more exciting.

• Your puppy will run happily toward you, and, as soon as she gets to you, give her a reward, whether it is food or a game.

• Move this training to the yard and practice calling her and making a big fuss when she comes. She may become distracted in the yard, with its different smells, so be patient and persevere with making yourself even more exciting.

When you start taking your Rottweiler out to the local park, it is best to use a training line, which is a lightweight leash considerably longer than a normal leash. They come in varying lengths; a line of around 10 to 15 feet (3 to 4.5 m) is ideal for recall training, as it prevents your dog from failing.

• Attach the training line to your dog's collar and allow her to wander off.

• After a short time, call her just as you did in the yard. If she comes running to you, reward as before and immediately let her go again. This way, she also learns that being recalled in the park does not mean the end of a walk.

• Get into the practice of taking hold of your Rottweiler's collar as she comes back and is rewarded, so that she never gets collar-shy. If you only hold her collar to put her back on a leash at the end of a walk, she'll soon begin to jump away as you reach down to her. By always taking hold of her collar when recalling her—and then letting her

go again—we can prevent this behavior (which is much easier than trying to correct it later!).

• If your Rottweiler ignores you when you have called her, simply pick up the training line to prevent her going out of range; this should attract her attention. Call her again, making yourself as exciting as possible, and reward her when she gets back to you.

By following this training method, as your Rottweiler passes through her different learning stages, you can keep her from going wrong. And, when regularly reinforced, the behavior you want will remain on cue for life.

Stationary exercises

These are easy to teach, and they can be used in many different situations, giving you good control over your dog.

Clicker training

This is a highly effective method of positive training, which can be used for all exercises and for all disciplines. The clicker is a small device that fits in the palm of your hand and makes a sharp clicking noise when pressed and released. The basic concept of clicker training is that the sound marks the correct behavior you are teaching, and the dog learns by the sound that she has done the right thing and can expect a reward.

To begin, your dog must learn that hearing a click means a reward is on the way. The best way to do this is to find a quiet area of your home that your dog is familiar with, and just click and give her a treat several times. Repeat this over a few days and she will quickly get the idea. You can test her understanding by clicking and seeing if she reacts to the sound by looking for food.

Sit

• Take a treat and hold it toward your puppy's nose. Slowly raise the treat upward and slightly heading back over her head.

• As your puppy lifts her head to watch the treat, her bottom will naturally hit the floor, and you can click and reward.

• When she is doing this every time, you can begin to add the cue "sit" just as the puppy goes into position.

Never push down on your Rottweiler's bottom, as this could damage her hips or joints, and, by placing her into position, she will never learn for herself. It is like teaching a child to tie his shoelaces: If you always tie them for him, he will never learn how to do it.

Down

This is probably one of the most important exercises you can teach your Rottweiler. A reliable instant down could one day save her life if she is running toward a road.

• Hold a treat in your closed hand, place the hand, palm down, on the floor, and wait.

• Your puppy will put her nose to your hand to smell the treat. Eventually, she will flop down to continue sniffing. As soon as she does, click and open your hand to reveal the treat.

• As with the "sit" exercise, once she is lying down regularly, begin to add the "down" cue when she is in the correct position.

This exercise can progress by teaching instant downs, which is done by throwing a treat for your dog and, when she has run to it and eaten it, cue her to "down" and click and reward when she does it. Keep it fun and light-hearted and your puppy will learn, seeing it as a game.

Control exercises

These exercises may not seem the most exciting, but they have double value. You are establishing control over your dog, which is important in a breed as big and powerful as the Rottweiler, and it teaches her to respect you. She must learn to inhibit her natural, exuberant behavior and do as you ask.

Stay

Once you have a reliable "sit" or "down," you can begin to teach the "stay" cue.

• Ask your puppy to "sit" or "down" and then count out loud to five. Your puppy should stay as you have left her, and the sound of your counting will distract her from moving.

• When you get to five, click and reward. Repeat and repeat.

• Progress by increasing your count to 10 and then 15, and so on. At this stage, introduce the "stay" cue before you start counting.

• Once you can count to 30, go back to counting to 10, but only count every other number out loud—that is, one, three, five—and gradually build up to 30.

• Continue using this method of reducing the numbers you say out loud until you can just give the "stay" cue.

The next step is to start increasing distance.

• Ask your puppy to "sit" or "down" and cue her to "stay." Then begin to count out loud and, at the same time, take a step or two away from her, then go straight back to her.

• As with the first part of the exercise, you can gradually build up distance by using the counting method.

If, at any time, your puppy gets

up, do not get angry with her; simply place her back in the "stay" position and start again. Never be afraid to go back a few stages to really cement her knowledge. Basic training is the foundation, and, as with buildings, a strong foundation will last.

Once you start to leave your dog in the "stay," always stand sideways in relation to her, so she doesn't think you are going to call her to come, and do not offer any eye contact. Keep the training periods short so your dog does not become bored and distracted.

Leave it

This is a very generalized cue that can be used not only to ask your dog to leave something that may have been dropped on the floor, but also to stop unwanted interaction with another dog.

• Make sure you have a high-level reward (such as a piece of sausage) in your hand, and a bowl with something less desirable (such as a dog biscuit).

• Put your puppy on a leash to prevent her from getting to the biscuit.

• Place the bowl close to your puppy, and, as she goes towards it, say, "leave it" in a strong, low voice. This should initially startle your puppy into looking at you.

• As soon as your Rottweiler looks at you, click and reward her with the high-level reward.

• Repeat this, using the leash to prevent the puppy from getting to the bowl. Never use a leash correction, as this is not necessary. She will quickly learn that "leave it" means "give eye contact and a tasty reward will follow."

It is very important that your puppy never gets what you are asking her to leave. So if you

have asked her to leave a biscuit, do not feed her that biscuit; take another out of the box.

Dog training tips

Many people teach this cue as a "wait" before allowing the dog to eat at mealtimes. However, "leave it" should be permanent, as you do not want your dog to leave something harmful for a short period of time only. Once a dog hears this cue, she should understand that it means "leave it forever."

This is a good cue to use when your Rottweiler reaches adolescence. Should she become aggressive toward other dogs, a firm "leave it" from the beginning will demonstrate that she cannot act this way. Always remember to give a high-value reward when she responds correctly.

Chapter 7

Keeping Your Rottweiler Busy

After you have successfully trained your dog on the basic skills, you can take her training a lot further with all kinds of organized canine sports. The Rottweiler is a highly intelligent breed and will relish the opportunity to use her brain.

A few of the most popular canine sports are listed here, but there are many more, including working trials just for Rottweilers. The American Kennel Club and United States Rottweiler Club (both listed in Find Out More) are good places to learn about sports for Rottweilers.

Canine Good Citizen

The American Kennel Club runs the Canine Good Citizen program. It promotes responsible ownership and helps you to train a well-behaved dog who will fit in with the community.

The program tests your dog on basic good manners, alone and with other people and dogs around. It's excellent for all pet owners

and is also an ideal starting point if you plan to compete with your Rottweiler in any sport when she is older.

Agility

Agility is basically a canine obstacle course. It is fast and furious and is great for the fitness of both handler and dog. And it can be quite addictive! The obstacles include hurdles, long jump, tire jump, tunnels (rigid and collapsible), weaving poles, an A-frame, a dog-walk, and a seesaw.

Agility is judged on the time taken to get around the course, with faults given for missing or knocking over obstacles, or taking the obstacles in the wrong order.

Puppies should not be allowed to do any agility exercises that

involve jumping or contact equipment until at least 12 months old. But while you are waiting, you can begin to teach your dog how to weave, introduce her to tunnels, and play around the jumps and poles so that she becomes familiar with the equipment.

Showing

If you decide that you would like to have a go at dog showing, you can start at a very early age with ring classes and fun matches for puppies from three months old. You will need to find a local club where there are people who know how the show scene works. It is best to start at the smaller, informal shows, before moving on to bigger shows for all breeds, then breed club or specialty shows. If you are determined enough, and your dog is good enough, you can compete in championship shows, where you may even achieve the dream of making your Rottweiler a show champion.

Obedience

If your dog is keen to learn the cues you started teaching her as a puppy, she might enjoy competitive obedience. The levels start off being relatively easy and become progressively more challenging, with additional exercises and increasingly minimal instructions from the handler.

Schutzhund

Schutzhund tests a dog in tracking, obedience, and protection work. The dog must track footsteps over mixed terrain, change direction, and show absolute accuracy and commitment to finding the track. She must also find dropped articles. Obedience is similar to the more advanced stages of competitive obedience trials. There is heeling, both on and off leash. The sit, down, stand, and stay are also done. The dog must retrieve a dumbbell over a jump and a wall. Some exercises require the dog to work under the noise of a firing gun.

In protection work, the dog must show heart and courage, but also must be under complete control and never bite the trial helper unless either the dog or the handler is attacked. Then she must attack fully and without hesitation, but must also stop biting on the command of the handler and guard the trial helper without any further aggression.

The ideal Rottweiler owner

The Rottweiler is a powerful, intelligent dog with a mind of her own. Things go wrong when people take on this breed without sufficient knowledge or experience. The ideal owner should:

• Work out a comprehensive program of socialization, giving their dog the opportunity to meet people of all ages, to interact with other dogs of sound temperament, and to be exposed to a wide variety of different situations.

• Allocate time for basic training and then find an outlet for the Rottweiler's mental energies. Ideally, this would entail further training in one of the canine sports, but it could be something as simple as teaching your dog tricks to do at home.

• Be firm but fair, and remain consistent in all dealings with your Rottweiler, so that she understands her place in the family.

Chapter 8

Health Care for Rottweilers

We are fortunate that the Rottweiler is a healthy dog, with no physical exaggerations, as you see in some breeds. With good routine care, a well-balanced diet, and sufficient exercise, most dogs will have few health problems.

However, it is your responsibility to put a program of preventive health care in place—and this should start from the moment your puppy, or adult dog, arrives in her new home.

Parasites

No matter how well you look after your Rottweiler you will have to accept that parasites—internal and external—are ever present, and you need to take preventive action.

Internal parasites live inside your dog. These are the various worms. Most will find a home in the digestive tract, but there is also a parasite that lives in the heart. If infestation is unchecked, a dog's

Vaccination Program

The American Animal Hospital Association and the American Veterinary Medical Association have issued vaccination guidelines that apply to all breeds of dogs. They divide the available vaccines into two groups: core vaccines, which every dog should get, and non-core vaccines, which are optional.

Core vaccines are canine parvovirus-2, distemper, and adenovirus-2. Puppies should get vaccinated every three to four weeks between the ages of 6 and 16 weeks, with the final dose at 14 to 16 weeks of age. If a dog older than 16 weeks is getting their first vaccine, one dose is enough. Dogs who received an initial dose at less than 16 weeks should be given a booster after one year, and then every three years or more thereafter.

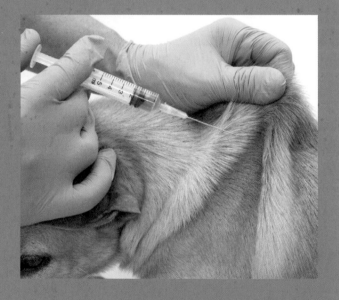

Rabies is also a core vaccine. For puppies less than 16 weeks old, a single dose should be given no earlier than 12 weeks of age. Revaccination is recommended annually or every three years, depending on the vaccine used and state and local laws.

Non-core vaccines are canine parainfluenza virus, Bordetella bronchiseptica, canine influenza virus, canine measles, leptospirosis, and Lyme disease.

The dog's exposure risk, lifestyle, and geographic location all come into play when deciding which non-core vaccines may be appropriate for your dog. Have a conversation with your veterinarian about the right vaccine protocol for your dog.

health will be severely jeopardized, but routine preventive treatmentis simple and effective.External parasites live on your dog's body—in her skin and fur, and sometimes in her ears.

Roundworm

This is found in the small intestine. Signs of infestation will be a poor coat, a potbelly, diarrhea, and lethargy. Prospective mothers should be treated before mating, but it is almost inevitable that parasites she may have will be passed on to the puppies. For this reason, a breeder will start a worming program, which you will need to continue. Ask your vet for advice on treatment, which will need to continue throughout your dog's life.

Tapeworm

Infection occurs when the dog ingests fleas or lice. The adult worm takes up residence in the small intestine, releasing mobile segments (which contain eggs), which can be seen in a dog's feces as small rice-like grains. The only other obvious sign of infestation is irritation of the anus. Again, routine preventive treatment is required throughout your Rottweiler's life.

Heartworm

This parasite is transmitted by mosquitoes, and is found in all parts of the USA, although its prevalence does vary. Heartworms live in the right side of the heart and larvae can grow up to 14 inches (35 cm) long. A dog with heartworm is at severe risk from heart failure, so preventive treatment, as advised by your vet, is essential. Dogs living in the USA should also have regular tests to check for the presence of infection.

Lungworm

Lungworm is a parasite that lives in the heart and major blood vessels supplying the lungs. It can cause many problems, such as breathing difficulties, excessive bleeding, sickness, diarrhea, seizures, and even death. The dog becomes infected when ingesting slugs and snails, often accidentally when rummaging through undergrowth. Lungworm is not common, but it is on the increase and a responsible owner should be aware of it. Fortunately, it is easily preventable, and even affected dogs usually make a full recovery if treated early enough. Your vet will be able to advise you on the risks in your area and what form of treatment may be required.

Fleas

A dog may carry many types of fleas. The flea stays on the dog only long enough to feed and breed, but its presence will result in itching. If your dog has an allergy to fleas—usually a reaction to the flea's saliva—she will scratch herself until she is raw. Spot-ons and chewable flea preventives are easy to use and highly effective, and should be given regularly to prevent fleas entirely. Some also prevent ticks.

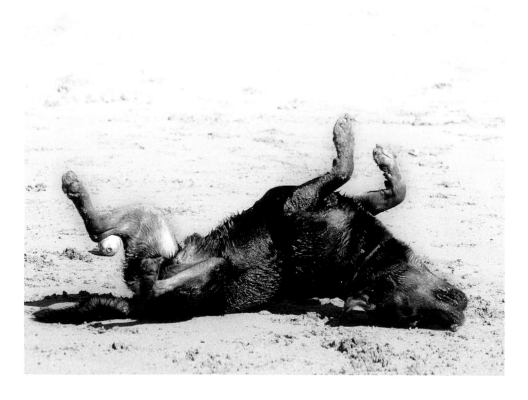

If your dog does have fleas, talk to your veterinarian about the best treatment. Bear in mind that your entire home, dog's whole environment, and all other pets in your home will also need to be treated.

Ticks

These are blood-sucking parasites that are most frequently found in areas where sheep or deer are present.

The main danger is their ability to pass a wide variety of very serious diseases—including Lyme disease—to both dogs and humans. The preventive you give your dog for fleas generally works for ticks, but you should discuss the best product to use with your veterinarian.

Ear mites

These parasites live in the outer ear canal. The signs of infestation are a brown, waxy discharge, and your dog will often shake her head and scratch her ear.

If you suspect your Rottweiler has ear mites, a visit to the vet will be needed so that medicated ear drops can be prescribed.

Cheyletiella mange

These small, white mites are visible to the naked eye and are often referred to as "walking dandruff." They cause a scruffy coat and mild itchiness. They are zoonotic—transferable to humans—so

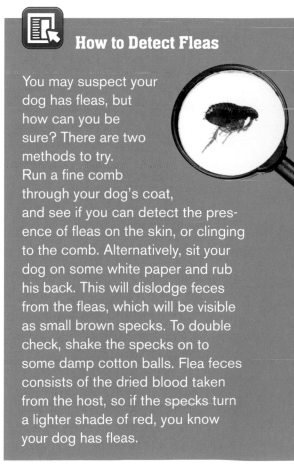

How to Detect Fleas

You may suspect your dog has fleas, but how can you be sure? There are two methods to try. Run a fine comb through your dog's coat, and see if you can detect the presence of fleas on the skin, or clinging to the comb. Alternatively, sit your dog on some white paper and rub his back. This will dislodge feces from the fleas, which will be visible as small brown specks. To double check, shake the specks on to some damp cotton balls. Flea feces consists of the dried blood taken from the host, so if the specks turn a lighter shade of red, you know your dog has fleas.

prompt treatment with an insecticide prescribed by your veterinarian is essential.

Chiggers

These are picked up from the undergrowth, and can be seen as bright red, yellow, or orange specks on the webbing between the toes, although this can also be found elsewhere on the body, such as on the ear flaps. Treatment is effective with the appropriate insecticide, prescribed by your vet.

Skin mites

There are two types of parasite that burrow into a dog's skin. Demodex canis is transferred from a mother to her pups while they are feeding. Treatment is with a topical preparation, and sometimes antibiotics are needed. Refer to your vet.

The other skin mite is sarcoptes scabiei, which causes intense itching and hair loss. It is highly contagious, so all dogs in a household will need to be treated, which involves repeated bathing with a medicated shampoo.

Common ailments

As with all living animals, dogs can be affected by a variety of ailments, most of which

How to Remove a Tick

If you spot a tick on your dog, do not try to pluck it off as you risk leaving the hard mouth parts embedded in his skin. The best way to remove a tick is to use a fine pair of tweezers or you can buy a tick remover. Grasp the tick head firmly and then pull the tick straight out from the skin. If you are using a tick remover, check the instructions, as some recommend a circular twist when pulling. When you have removed the tick, clean the area with mild soap and water.

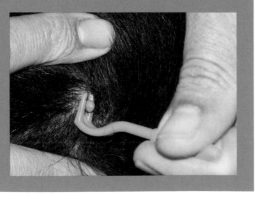

can be treated effectively after consulting with your vet, who will prescribe appropriate medication and will advise you on how to care for your dog's needs.

Here are some of the more common problems that could affect your Rottweiler, with advice on how to deal with them.

Anal glands

These are two small sacs on either side of the anus, which produce a dark brown secretion. The anal glands should empty every time a dog defecates, but if they become blocked or impacted, a dog will experience increasing discomfort. She may lick at her rear end, or scoot her bottom along the ground to relieve the irritation.

Treatment involves a trip to the vet, who will empty the glands manually. It is important to do this without delay or they could become infected.

Dental problems

Good dental hygiene will do much to minimize problems with gum infection and tooth decay. If tartar accumulates to the extent that you cannot remove it by brushing, your dog will need to be anesthetized for a dental cleaning by the veterinarian.

Diarrhea

There are many reasons why a dog has diarrhea, but most commonly it is the result of scavenging, a sudden change of diet, or an adverse reaction to a particular type of food.

If your dog is suffering from diarrhea, the first step is to withhold food for a day. It is important that she does not become dehydrated, so make sure that fresh drinking water is available. However, drinking too much can increase the diarrhea, which may be accompanied with vomiting, so limit how much she drinks at any one time.

After allowing the stomach to rest, feed a bland diet, such as white fish or chicken with boiled rice for a few days. In most cases, your dog's motions will return to normal and you can resume normal feeding, although this should be done gradually.

However, if this fails to work and the diarrhea persists for more than a few days, you should consult your vet. Your dog may have an infection, which needs to be treated with antibiotics, or the diarrhea may indicate some other problem that needs expert diagnosis.

Ear problems

The Rottweiler's ears lie close to her head, so air cannot circulate as freely as it would in a dog with ears that stand up. Therefore, it is important to check them regularly.

A healthy ear is clean, with no sign of redness or inflammation, and no evidence of a waxy brown discharge or a foul odor. If you see

your dog scratching her ear, shaking her head, or holding one ear at an odd angle, you will need to consult your vet. The most likely causes are ear mites, an infection, or there may be a foreign body, such as a grass seed, trapped in the ear. Depending on the cause, treatment is with medicated ear drops, possibly containing antibiotics. If a foreign body is suspected, the vet will need look further.

Eye problems

The Rottweiler's eyes are set square in her skull; they do not protrude, as in breeds such as the Pug, so they are less vulnerable to injury. However, if your Rottweiler's eyes look red and sore, she may be suffering from conjunctivitis. This may or may not be accompanied with a watery or a crusty discharge. Conjunctivitis can be caused by a bacterial or viral infection, it could be the result of an injury, or it may be a reaction to pollen.

Conjunctivitis may also be the first sign of more serious inherited eye problems, which will be discussed later in this chapter. Sore and inflamed eyes may also be the result of a foreign body, such as a grass seed, entering the eye.

You will need to consult your veterinarian for a correct diagnosis, but in the case of an infection, treatment with medicated eye drops is effective.

Foreign bodies

In the home, puppies—and some older dogs—cannot resist chewing anything that looks interesting. Even when she is only a puppy, a Rottweiler has powerful jaws, and when she has her adult

teeth, she can be very destructive.

The toys you choose for your dog should be suitably robust to withstand damage, but children's toys can be irresistible. Some dogs will chew—and swallow—anything from socks and other items from the laundry basket, to golf balls and stones from the yard. Obviously, these items are indigestible and could cause an obstruction in your dog's intestines, which is potentially lethal.

The signs to look for are vomiting and a tucked-up posture. The dog will often be restless and will look as if she is in pain. In this situation, you must get your dog to the vet without delay, as surgery will be needed to remove the obstruction.

The other type of foreign body that may cause problems is grass seed. A grass seed can enter an orifice such as a nostril, down an ear, the gap between the eye and the eyelid, or it can penetrate the soft skin between the toes. It can also be swallowed.

The introduction of a foreign body induces a variety of symptoms, depending on the point of entry and where it travels to. The signs to look for include head shaking, ear scratching, the eruption of an abscess, sore, inflamed eyes, or a persistent cough. The vet will be able to make a proper diagnosis, and surgery may be required.

As a preventive measure, avoid exercising your Rottweiler in areas of long grass when it is seeding, and if she strays into grassland, groom her and examine her thoroughly when you return home.

Heatstroke

The Rottweiler is a heavyweight breed, and has a tendency to overheat. When the temperature rises, make sure your dog always has access to shady areas, and wait for a cooler part of the day before going for a walk. Be extra careful if you leave your Rottweiler in the car, as the temperature can rise dramatically even on a cloudy day. Heatstroke can happen very rapidly, and unless you are able lower your dog's temperature, it can be fatal.

The signs of heatstroke include heavy panting and difficulty breathing, bright red tongue and mucous membranes, thick saliva, and vomiting. Eventually, the dog becomes progressively unsteady and passes out.

If your Rottweiler appears to be suffering from heatstroke, this is a true emergency. Lie her flat and then cool her as quickly as possible by hosing her or covering her with wet towels. As soon as she has made some recovery, take her to the vet.

Gastric dilatation/volvulus

This condition, commonly known as bloat or gastric torsion, is occurs when the stomach swells visibly (dilatation) and then rotates (volvulus), so that the exit into the small intestine becomes blocked, preventing food from leaving. This results in stomach pain and a bloated abdomen. It is a severe, life-threatening condition that requires immediate veterinary attention (usually surgery) to decompress and return the stomach to its normal position.

Rottweilers may be at risk, as it is usually seen in large deep-chested breeds. Greedy, fast-eating dogs may be more susceptible, and this is further compounded by exercise immediately before or after eating. It's best not to exercise your Rottweiler an hour before feeding, and wait for two hours after feeding before allowing exercise.

If your Rottweiler has a tendency to bolt her food, you can buy a special bowl that is designed to make a dog eat more slowly. These are available in most pet supply stores.

Lameness/limping

There are a wide variety of reasons why a dog might go lame, from a simple muscle strain to a fracture, ligament damage, or more complex problems with the joints, including inherited disorders. It takes an expert to make a correct diagnosis, so if you are concerned about your dog, do not delay in seeking help.

As your Rottweiler becomes elderly, she may suffer from arthritis, which you will see as general stiffness, particularly when she gets up after resting. It will help if you ensure her bed is in a warm, draft-free location, and if your Rottweiler gets wet after exercise, you must dry her thoroughly.

If your elderly Rottweiler seems to be in pain, consult your vet, who will be able to help with pain relief medication and nutritional supplements.

Lumps

As your Rottweiler gets older, you may notice small lumps appearing on her body. These are usually benign, but there is a possibility that it could be malignant. Regardless of your Rottweiler's age, any lumps that you notice should be examined by your vet, who may advise taking a sample to be checked by a pathologist.

Skin problems

If your dog is scratching or nibbling at her skin, the first thing to check for is fleas. There are other external parasites that also cause itching and hair loss, but you will need a vet to help you find the culprit.

Acute moist dermatitis, also known as hot spot, may occur when a dog keeps scratching an area and the skin becomes wet and infected. A course of antibiotic treatment will be required.

An allergic reaction is another major cause of skin problems, resulting in a condition known as atopy. This is a hypersensitivity to environmental allergens such as pollens, dust mites, or molds. Initial signs are localized licking, itching, and reddening of skin, and may progress to generalized self-trauma, secondary infection, scaling, and crusting.

Treatment may involve steroids, antibiotics, and even desensitization vaccines, following skin testing to determine the causative allergen.

Dogs can also have reactions to ingredients in their food—most often proteins. This may result in chronic diarrhea, intolerance of certain foods, itchy skin, or sore ears. The clinical signs often vary in severity. Diagnosis involves strict food trials.

Inherited disorders

The Rottweiler does have a few breed-related disorders. If your dog is diagnosed with any of the diseases listed here, it is important to remember that they can affect offspring, so it is not wise to breed affected dogs. There are now recognized screening tests to enable breeders to check for carrier and affected individuals, and hence reduce the prevalence of these diseases within the breed. DNA testing is also becoming more widely available, and as research into the different genetic diseases progresses, more DNA tests are being developed.

Subaortic Stenosis

This is a hereditary disease, but testing of breeding stock is now doing much to reduce its incidence. This is a malformation of the aortic valve in the heart, and is present at birth.

Narrowing of the valve causes a murmur to be heard as the blood is pushed through the heart at a faster velocity than normal. This increased effort needed to push the blood through results in an growth in size of the left ventricle of the heart as the muscle works harder.

Diagnosis involves Doppler echocardiography, which can determine the flow rate of the blood through the valves of the heart. Rottweilers with mild forms of SAS can show no clinical signs. More severe forms are usually degenerative and heart failure will occur as the heart loses the ability to cope. Restricted exercise may help slow progression of the disease and medications can be prescribed to help the heart efficacy.

All breeding stock should be tested by a qualified cardiologist before matings are planned. Affected dogs should not be bred.

Canine acne

Also known as muzzle furunculosis, this presents as comedones (blackheads) and can progress to pustules and papules (infected spots) on the skin of the muzzle, which may be irritating and can become infected. Generally this is a self-limiting disease, but if the skin becomes infected or irritated, treatment with shampoo or antibiotics may be needed.

Eye disorders

There are three eye conditions that most commonly affect Rottweilers—entropion, ectropion, and progressive retinal atrophy (PRA). Testing for all three is carried out by the Canine Eye Registration Foundation in the USA.

Entropion is an inrolling of the eyelids, which may result in inflammation and infection. There may also be small, wart-like growths on the lids, which is not usually a problem unless they grow large or touch the cornea. More severe cases of entropion may require surgery.

Ectropion occurs when the eyelids roll outward. This is a condition that often improves with age, and surgery is rarely required.

PRA can cause progressive blindness in Rottweilers as young as one year of age, or it can develop later in life if the dog has inherited the disorder. It will become apparent the dog is having trouble seeing in semi-dark or complete darkness. There is no treatment.

Joint disorders

The Rottweiler is a large, fast-growing breed and, as a result, she is vulnerable to joint problems, particularly during the growing period. These may include the following.

Cruciate rupture

The cruciate ligaments of the stifle (knee) can be partially or completely torn when placed under a lot of physical stress, resulting in lameness. This condition is relatively common in Rottweilers, especially if they are overweight, which puts extra stress on the ligaments. Treatment often involves surgery, along with an extended period of rest, and the affected joint is prone to arthritis later in life.

Elbow dysplasia

This is a developmental disease where the elbow joint does not mature correctly. Signs of lameness are usually seen in younger, large-breed dogs.

Surgery may be indicated to correct the abnormalities, but the affected joints will be more prone to arthritis later in life.

There is an increased incidence of ED in Rottweilers, so it is essential that all breeding animals be tested. In the US, X-rays are submitted to the Orthopedic Foundation for Animals. Severely affected dogs should not be used for breeding.

Hip dysplasia

In dogs with this structural problem, the ball and socket joint of the hip develops incorrectly so that the head of the femur (ball) and the acetabulum of the pelvis (socket) do not fit snugly. This causes pain in the joint, and may be seen as lameness in dogs as young as five months old, with deterioration into severe arthritis over time. Gentle exercise, keeping the dog at a good weight, anti-inflammatory drugs, and home management are all part of the treatment. Severe cases may require surgery.

This disease can be screened for. X-rays are submitted to the Orthopedic Foundation for Animals or PennHIP, where they are graded according to the degree of hip laxity.

Hip dysplasia is thought to have a genetic component, but the mode of inheritance has not been established, since multiple genes are involved. Environmental factors, such as nutrition and rapid growth, may also play a role in its development.

Careful and responsible breeding over the years has reduced the prevalence of this disease in Rottweilers, but care must be taken to ensure that this continues into the future.

Osteochondrosis and osteochondritis dissecans (OCD)

Osteochondrosis results from abnormal growth of the cartilage on the ends of bones. A lack of blood supply to the bone tissue de-

stroys it, and the joint cartilage may become fragmented or pieces may come loose in the joint. This condition is typically seen in young, growing dogs, and can be very painful, especially if the fragment moves within the joint. Surgery may be needed to remove it.

Panosteitis

Inflammation of the long bones of the legs can occur in young large breed dogs. This causes clinical signs of lameness without an initiating cause, and it may shift among all four legs. Pain levels vary from mild to severe. If mild, most dogs are back to normal by two years of age, but if severe, anti-inflammatories and restricted exercise will be required.

Osteosarcoma

This is a bone cancer that affects Rottweilers. It is most commonly found in the long bones of the legs, but may also be found elsewhere in the skeleton. Initial clinical signs are lameness, swelling and pain, but may progress to fracture in more severe cases. Treatment to improve survival times may include surgery, chemotherapy, or radiation therapy.

Summing up

This has been a long list of health problems, but it was not my intention to scare you. Acquiring some basic knowledge is an asset, as it will allow you to spot signs of trouble at an early stage. Early diagnosis very often leads to the most effective treatment.

The Rottweiler as a breed is a healthy, energetic dog with a zest for life, and annual check-ups will be all she needs. As a companion, she will bring many happy memories in the years you will spend together.

Find Out More

Books

Bradshaw, John, *Dog Sense: How the New Science of Dog Behavior Can Make You a Better Friend to Your Pet*, New York: Basic Books, 2014.

Eldredge, Debra M., DVM, Liisa D. Carlson, DVM, Delbert G. Carlson, DVM, and James M. Giffin, MD, *Dog Owner's Home Veterinary Handbook*, 4th Ed. New York: Howell Book House, 2007.

Gerritsen, Resi, and Ruud Haak, *K9 Schutzhund Training: A Manual for IPO Training Through Positive Reinforcement*, 2nd Ed. Edmonton: Dog Training Press, 2014.

Stilwell, Victoria, *Train Your Dog Positively: Understand Your Dog and Solve Common Behavior Problems Including Separation Anxiety, Excessive Barking, Aggression, Housetraining, Leash Pulling, and More!* Berkeley: Ten Speed Press, 2013.

Websites

www.amrottclub.org American Rottweiler Club

www.akc.org American Kennel Club

www.petmd.com PetMD

www.ukcdogs.com United Kennel Club

www.usrconline.org United States Rottweiler Club

Series Glossary of Key Terms

agility   in this case, a canine sport in which dogs navigate an obstacle course

breed standard   a detailed written description of the ideal type, size, shape, colors, movement, and temperament of a dog breed

conforms   aligns with, agrees with

docked   cut or shortened

dysplasia   a structural problem with the joints, when the bones do not fit properly together

heatstroke   a medical condition in which the body overheats to a dangerous degree

muzzle   (n) the nose and mouth of a dog; (v) to place a restraint on the mouth of a dog

neuter   to make a male dog unable to create puppies

parasites   organisms that live and feed on a host organism

pedigree   the formal record of an animal's descent, usually showing it to be purebred

socialization   the process of introducing a dog to as many different sights, sounds, animals, people and experiences as possible, so he will feel comfortable with them all

spay   to make a female dog unable to create puppies

temperament   the basic nature of an animal, especially as it affects their behavior

Index